NEW PERSPECTIVES

Hiroshima and Nagasaki

R. G. GRANT

WAYLAND

First published in 1997 by
Wayland Publishers Ltd,
61 Western Road,
Hove,
East Sussex BN3 1JD

This book was prepared for Wayland Publishers Ltd
by Ruth Nason.

Series editor: Alex Woolf
Series design: Stonecastle Graphics
Book design: LNbooks, Houghton Regis, Bedfordshire

Find Wayland on the internet at:
http://www.wayland.co.uk

British Library Cataloguing in Publication Data
Hiroshima & Nagasaki. - (New perspectives)
1. World War, 1939 - 1945 - Campaigns - Japan - Juvenile literature 2. Hiroshima-shi (Japan) - History - Bombardment, 1945 - Juvenile literature
I. Title
940.5'425

ISBN 0 7502 2052 X

Printed and bound in Italy by G. Canale & C.S.p.A., Turin

Cover photos: an atom bomb test, 1950s; a survivor of the Hiroshima bombing.

Page 1: Colonel Paul Tibbets, pilot of the plane which dropped the atom bomb on Hiroshima.

Acknowledgements

The Author and Publishers thank the following for their permission to reproduce photographs: Camera Press: pages 6b, 13, 19, 24, 28, 45, 49, 50; John Frost Historical Newspapers: pages 15b, 35, 42b, 44; Robert Harding Picture Library: page 57t; Hulton-Getty Picture Collection: pages 7, 10, 11b, 17, 20, 23, 32, 33, 43t, 48; Photri, Inc.: pages 31, 47; Popperfoto: pages 4, 12, 14, 15t, 16, 21, 22, 26, 29, 34, 36, 38, 42t, 43b, 51, 53, 55, 56, 58, 59; Topham Picturepoint: cover and pages 1, 3, 5, 6t, 8, 9, 18, 25, 30, 40, 52; TRIP/C. Rennie: page 57b.

CONTENTS

The Bombing of Hiroshima   4

Total War   10

Making the Atom Bomb   23

Deciding to Drop the Bomb   32

Nagasaki and Surrender   42

Living with the Bomb   50

Date List   60

Resources   61

Glossary   62

Index   63

Each year, in memory of the people killed by the bomb on Hiroshima, lanterns are floated on the river, past the remains of the Industry Promotion Centre.

THE BOMBING OF HIROSHIMA

On 6 August 1945, at 2.45 a.m. local time, a B-29 bomber of Group 509 of the United States Army Air Force lifted off from Tinian Island in the Marianas and headed out into the night over the Pacific Ocean. Watching from the floodlit airfield were a crowd of news photographers and cameramen, because this was a historic flight. The aircraft, commanded by Colonel Paul W. Tibbets, was going to drop a new kind of bomb, more destructive than anything seen before, on the Japanese city of Hiroshima.

The bomb was the world's first atomic bomb, but this was a secret known to very few people. Tibbets had been told, but not his crew. They knew that the mission was important. The USA and its allies had been fighting Japan for three and a half years. The crew had been told that America's new secret weapon might end the war in a single day.

The *Enola Gay* is now on display at the Smithsonian Air and Space Museum, Washington.

" A prayer before takeoff

Before the takeoff, Group 509's chaplain, William Downey, recited a special prayer for the success of the mission to bomb Hiroshima. He prayed that God would protect the air crew and that 'armed with Thy might they may bring this war to a rapid end.' Downey believed that, although killing was wrong, in war:

'killing is the name of the game; those who don't accept that have to be prepared to accept the alternative – defeat.' (Quoted in Thomas and Morgan-Witts, *Ruin from Air*) "

Tibbets had nicknamed the aircraft Enola Gay, his mother's maiden name. It was not alone on its mission. Three planes flew in advance, to report back on weather conditions over Japan, and two other aircraft accompanied the *Enola Gay* to its target. The 2,400-kilometre flight was uneventful. The crew drank coffee and ate ham sandwiches. At 6.30 a.m. Japanese time, the massive bomb was primed. Forty-five minutes later, the weather aircraft reported that conditions over Hiroshima were good.

By this stage in the war, Japan had virtually no air defences. The *Enola Gay* approached its target flying at 9,500 metres and at a speed of 320 kilometres per hour. At 8.14 a.m. Tibbets ordered his crew to put on polaroid goggles, to protect their eyes. At 8.15 a.m. the B-29 arrived over its aiming point, the Aioi Bridge in the centre of Hiroshima. A minute later, the atom bomb airburst over the city.

Unlike most urban areas in Japan, Hiroshima had not yet been heavily bombed. It expected to be, since it was an important port and industrial centre. There were about 320,000 people in the city on that day. It was a still, warm summer morning. The streets were busy with people walking and cycling to work. Soldiers were doing physical exercises in the open air. Thousands of schoolgirls were also outdoors, working to make firebreaks between buildings. Many looked up to see the three shiny silver B-29s high in the blue sky.

After the explosion, the crew of the *Enola Gay* saw smoke spread out over Hiroshima and a mushroom cloud form high above it.

Hiroshima is situated on the southern coast of Japan's largest island, Honshu, where the river Ohta discharges into the sea. The bomb was dropped on the Aioi bridge, which crossed one of the channels of the river delta.

The first flash of the explosion was as bright as a thousand suns. The heat and light killed or maimed thousands of people in less than a second. Those nearest the centre of the explosion were vaporized or burned to a cinder. All that was left of some was a shadow on a wall. Further away people had their hair and their skin burned off. Many were blinded. Their clothes fused to their bodies.

The blast that followed the flash demolished houses and factories, tossed trams and trains about like toys, and blackened the sun with dust and debris. The explosion set up violent winds that created firestorms. Ringed by fire, thousands of people jumped into the river to avoid burning, and were drowned.

Left: A victim of the atom bomb.
Right: In a makeshift hospital, October, 1945.

Survivors of Hiroshima

Futaba Kitayama, a Japanese woman, was in Hiroshima when the atom bomb exploded:

'... a shattering flash filled the sky. I was thrown to the ground and the world collapsed around me ... I couldn't see anything. It was completely dark ... When I finally struggled free there was a terrible smell and I rubbed my mouth with a towel I carried around my waist. All the skin came off my face, and then all the skin on my arms and hands fell off. The sky was black as night, and I ran homewards towards the Tsurumi river bridge. People by the hundreds were flailing in the river ...'
(Quoted in Harper, *Miracle of Deliverance*)

A survivor who was only five years old at the time later remembered the same horror:

'People came fleeing from the nearby streets ... they were almost unrecognizable. The skin was burned off some of them and was hanging from their hands and from their chins; their faces were red and so swollen that you could hardly tell where their eyes and mouths were ...'
(Quoted in Rhodes, *The Making of the Atomic Bomb*)

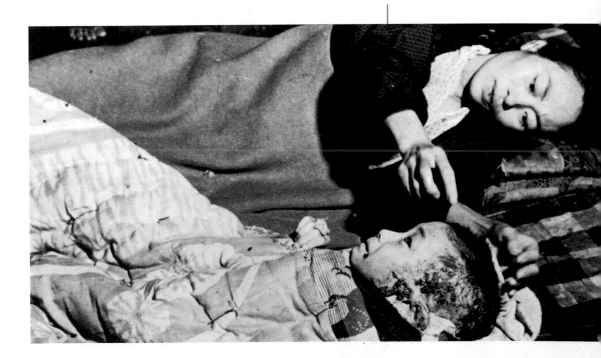

The bomber crew's reactions

About an hour before the bomb was dropped, Tibbets announced to his crew that they were carrying the world's first atomic bomb. He told them that when it was dropped, their reactions would be taped, for history.

The plane's tail gunner, Sergeant Robert Caron, described what he saw:

'Fires are springing up everywhere, like flames shooting out of a huge bed of coals ... The mushroom is spreading out. It's maybe a mile or two wide and half a mile high ... The city must be below that. The flames and smoke are billowing out, whirling out into the foothills ...'

The radar officer, Lt. Jacob Beser, commented:

'It's pretty terrific. What a relief it worked.'

Later, the navigator, Theodore Van Kirk, remembered thinking:

'Thank God the war is over and I don't have to get shot at any more. I can go home.'

Left to right: Major Thomas Ferebee, the bombardier; Colonel Paul Tibbets, the pilot; Captain Theodore Van Kirk, the navigator; and Captain Robert Lewis, the co-pilot. They and the rest of the crew received a heroes' welcome when they landed back on Tinian Island at 2.58 p.m.

No one will ever know exactly how many people were killed in Hiroshima on 6 August 1945. It is most often said that about 80,000 people died either of the immediate effects of the bomb or of exposure to gamma radiation, which killed victims in twenty to thirty days. But the Hiroshima city government says that the true death toll was 140,000 by the end of 1945. An area of the city about 10 kilometres across was devastated.

When the American President, Harry S. Truman, was told of the success of the *Enola Gay*'s mission, he was jubilant, describing it as 'the greatest thing in history'. Later, in a statement to the American people, he warned the Japanese of worse to come: 'If they do not accept our terms, they can expect a rain of ruin from the air the like of which has never been seen on this earth.'

The remains of a wrist watch found in the ruins of Hiroshima. The shadows of the hands had been burned on to the face at 8.16 a.m.

A ghoulish celebration

Atomic scientist Otto Frisch was one of the team who had created the bomb. He and his colleagues heard the news at Los Alamos, New Mexico:

'Somebody opened my door and shouted, "Hiroshima has been destroyed!"; about a hundred thousand people were thought to have been killed. I still remember the feeling of unease, indeed nausea, when I saw how many of my friends were rushing ... to celebrate. Of course they were exalted by the success of their work, but it seemed rather ghoulish to celebrate the sudden death of a hundred thousand people, even if they were "enemies".'
(Quoted in Rhodes, *The Making of the Atomic Bomb*)

TOTAL WAR

By the time the atom bomb was dropped on Hiroshima, around 50 million people had died in the Second World War. It was already the most destructive war in human history. Devastation of cities and mass killing of civilians had become almost commonplace.

The war started in Europe. In Germany, the Nazi dictator Adolf Hitler came to power in 1933. He built up the German army and bullied Germany's neighbours. When Hitler invaded Poland on 1 September 1939, Britain and France, the leading democratic countries in Europe, declared war on Germany. At first the German armies swept all before them. The Germans defeated France and conquered most of Europe. In June 1941, they invaded the Soviet Union. US President Franklin D. Roosevelt supplied arms to help Britain fight the Nazis. But for two years, the USA stayed out of the fighting.

The USA enters the war

It was Japan that brought the USA into the war. The official ruler of Japan was Emperor Hirohito, but real power in the country lay with the Japanese army and navy officers. In the 1930s Japan's military leaders began to build an Asian empire. They invaded China in 1937

December 1937. Japanese invaders of China wrote the name of their army unit on this antique Chinese gun.

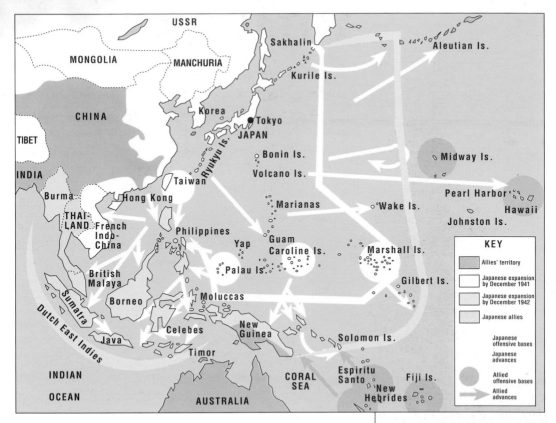

Japanese expansion, 1941-2.

and in 1940 they began to take over parts of South-east Asia. General Tojo Hideki, a leading militarist, became Japanese prime minister.

President Roosevelt and British Prime Minister Winston Churchill wanted to stop Japanese expansion. They knew Japan's war machine depended on imported oil. In the summer of 1941 they cut off the supply of oil to Japan, putting a block on the country's imports. The Japanese military leaders decided to go to war.

US President Roosevelt and British Prime Minister Winston Churchill at a meeting in the Atlantic in August 1941.

On 7 December 1941, Japanese aircraft made a surprise attack on the US naval base at Pearl Harbor in Hawaii. They sank four American battleships and killed around 3,500 US servicemen. This 'sneak' attack, before an official declaration of war, shocked the American people. The following day, the USA and Britain declared war on Japan.

American battleships on fire after the Japanese attack on Pearl Harbor. President Roosevelt called the day of the attack 'a date which will live in infamy'. The phrase 'Remember Pearl Harbor' became a motto for American troops throughout the war.

On 11 December, Hitler and his Italian ally, Benito Mussolini, declared war on the USA. So, in Europe, an alliance of the USA, Britain and the Soviet Union (the Allies) fought Germany and Italy. And in the Pacific, the USA and Britain – with its Commonwealth – fought Japan. The Soviet Union did not join in the war against Japan until the very end.

The British and American leaders declared a policy of 'unconditional surrender'. This meant that they would not allow Germany or Japan to negotiate peace terms. To end the war, both enemy countries would have to accept defeat and allow the Allies to do whatever they wanted with them.

Hatred of the Japanese

People normally feel hatred for their enemies in war. But in the Second World War the Americans hated the Japanese to an extreme degree – far more than they hated the Germans or Italians.

Pearl Harbor started this feeling. Hatred of Japan then increased as news spread of Japanese war crimes. In their early victories, the Japanese took many Allied prisoners. These men were often starved, beaten, tortured or killed. In the Philippines, many thousands of US and Filipino prisoners died on the infamous Bataan Death March in April 1942. They were killed by brutal treatment, executions, hunger and disease. About 15,000 British, Australian and other Allied prisoners died working on the Burma railway (portrayed in the famous film *The Bridge on the River Kwai*). In all, about one in four Allied prisoners of the Japanese died in captivity.

These prisoners of the Japanese were freed by Allied troops from a gaol in Singapore.

Remember Pearl Harbor

Journalist William T. Laurence flew on the mission that dropped a second atom bomb, on the city of Nagasaki, on 9 August 1945. In an article in the *New York Times* three weeks after the event, he described his feelings as he had looked down on the city about to be destroyed:

'Does one feel any pity or compassion for the poor devils about to die? Not when one thinks of Pearl Harbor and the Bataan Death March.'

The Japanese bombing of Shanghai in China in 1937 caused terrible destruction.

The Japanese 'viper'

In February 1942 President Roosevelt signed Executive Order 9066. Under this order, 110,000 people of Japanese origin, many of them full American citizens, were forcibly removed from states on the west coast of the USA. They were herded into camps in the mid-west. This action was taken against Japanese Americans but not against German or Italian Americans. White Americans felt that the Japanese were a strange, alien race. The *Los Angeles Times* wrote at the time:

'A viper is nonetheless a viper wherever the egg is hatched – so a Japanese American, born of Japanese parents, grows up to be a Japanese not an American.'

US Secretary of War Henry Stimson wrote in his diary:

'Their racial characteristics are such we cannot understand or trust even the citizen Japanese [Japanese who had become American citizens].'

The Japanese were just as brutal towards fellow Asians. For example, about 60,000 Koreans died working as slave labourers in Japan. Asian women were forced to work as sex slaves in Japanese army brothels. One of the worst massacres of the war happened in Manila, the capital of the Philippines, in 1945. A Filipino, Carlos Romulo, described seeing 'tortured bodies ... pushed into heaps on the Manila streets, their hands tied behind their backs, and bayonet stabs running through and through.'

Shanghai, 1937: this Chinese man and his granddaughter were among the thousands left homeless as the Japanese invaded and defeated China.

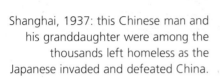

FOR MURDER, BARBARISM AND INHUMANITY

From the *Daily Mirror*, 31 January 1944. British and US wartime propaganda showed the Japanese as evil aggressors.

66 Kill all Japanese

An opinion poll carried out in the USA in December 1944 asked ordinary Americans: 'What do you think we should do with Japan as a country after the war?'

One in three people answered that Japan should cease to exist as a country. More than one in eight said that all the Japanese should be killed. US soldiers felt even more strongly. In an opinion poll in 1943, a half of US soldiers said that all the Japanese would have to be killed before there could be peace. 99

War without limits

The Second World War was a 'total war', fought without any limits. Britain and the USA believed they were fighting for freedom against slavery, and for civilization against barbarism. They felt they were justified in doing anything to defeat such evil enemies as Germany and Japan.

An example of total war was the bombing of civilians far away from the battle front. Japan had bombed Chinese cities before the Second World War. In the early years of the war, German aircraft bombed Warsaw, Rotterdam, London and many other European cities. Britain and the USA bombed cities in Germany and Japan, although they knew that thousands of ordinary men, women and children would be killed.

One argument made for bombing cities was that it would destroy the industries that produced arms and other material for the war. Another was that it would break the enemy's will to fight. Most ordinary Americans and Britons were pleased that German and Japanese cities were bombed, although there were some protests when the RAF killed 60,000 people in an air raid on Dresden, Germany, in February 1945.

Bomb damage in London, May 1941.

An American B-29 plane dropping bombs on Okayama, a Japanese base, in 1944.

The bombing of civilians

Before the war, both President Roosevelt and the US Secretary of War, Henry L. Stimson, spoke out against the bombing of civilians. On 1 September 1939, President Roosevelt condemned the use of air attack against towns and cities:

'The ruthless bombing from the air of civilians ... during the past few years, which has resulted in the maiming and in the death of thousands of defenceless men, women and children, has ... profoundly shocked the conscience of humanity.'
(Quoted in Rhodes, *The Making of the Atomic Bomb*)

Having come in to the war, the USA never officially changed its policy of bombing only military targets. American leaders sometimes used self-deception to protect their principles. In March 1945, after a fire-bomb attack on Tokyo killed around 100,000 civilians, Stimson asked his airforce commanders to assure him that they had only been attacking military targets.

A Japanese suicide plane attacks the USS *Missouri*, 8 May 1945.

Fighting to the death

The fighting in the Pacific was fierce and merciless. The Japanese were schooled to die for their emperor and country and therefore would resist to the last man. In 1942, triumphant Japanese armies spread as far as Burma, Indonesia and Papua New Guinea. Then the Americans drove them back island by island across the Pacific. As the fighting drew closer to Japan, American deaths increased. So did the readiness of the Japanese to die rather than surrender. When the island of Saipan fell to the Americans in July 1944, Japanese officers ordered Japanese civilians on the island to commit suicide rather than surrender. Whole families obeyed. Many leaped from cliff tops into the sea before the startled eyes of US soldiers and pressmen.

At the battle of Leyte Gulf in October 1944, Japanese airmen began using 'kamikaze' suicide tactics. They turned their aircraft into flying bombs, crashing into

No surrender

Taking the island of Iwo Jima from the Japanese in February to March 1945, 6,800 US marines were killed and 21,900 wounded. Japanese policy was: No surrender. General Tadimichi Kuribayashi, the Japanese commander on Iwo Jima, told his men:

'We shall grasp bombs, charge the enemy tanks and destroy them ... Each man will make it his duty to kill ten of the enemy before dying.' (Quoted in Rhodes, *The Making of the Atomic Bomb*)

Of 26,000 Japanese soldiers on the island, only 1,000 were taken prisoner. The other 25,000 were killed.

the decks of Allied warships. The suicidal courage of the Japanese made the Americans more ruthless in response. US Admiral William Halsey, one of the commanders in the Pacific, had the motto: 'Kill Japs, kill Japs, kill more Japs.'

Tokyo burns

In January 1945 Major-General Curtis LeMay took command of US air attacks on Japan. He ordered 20th Bomber Command to carry out a mass raid with fire-bombs – incendiaries – on the Japanese capital, Tokyo. The buildings of Tokyo were very close together and made of wood and paper. On the night of 9-10 March a raid by more than 300 aircraft started a fire that destroyed 39 square kilometres of the city. More than 100,000 people are thought to have died.

The official US Strategic Bombing Survey said, after the war, that 'probably more people lost their lives by fire at Tokyo in a six hour period than at any time in the history of man.'

Major-General Curtis LeMay.

A view of Tokyo after the US air raid in March 1945. Only modern steel and concrete buildings were left intact.

Okinawa

The fighting in the Pacific reached its peak on the island of Okinawa from April to June 1945. The Americans fought for three months to take the island. About 12,500 Americans were killed and 36,500 wounded. Around 110,000 Japanese soldiers died and almost as many civilians. Some Japanese civilians who refused to commit suicide rather than surrendering to the Americans were killed by their own soldiers.

The closing months

While the battle in Okinawa was being fought, events elsewhere in the world moved fast. On 12 April President Roosevelt died. His vice-president, Harry S. Truman, became the new US president. On 30 April, with troops of the Soviet Union already in Berlin, Adolf Hitler killed himself. Germany surrendered the following week. Meanwhile, in Japan, a new government led by Baron Suzuki Kantaro took office.

An American soldier reads the news of the German surrender, May 1945.

The Japanese leaders knew that they had really lost the war. The Japanese economy relied utterly on imports of food and fuel. An American sea blockade had cut Japanese trade to almost nothing. The country faced starvation and the collapse of its transport system and its industries. Japan's cities were being battered and burned to dust and ashes by mass air raids – Major-General Curtis LeMay reckoned that by September there would be no targets left worth bombing.

But the Japanese military commanders still insisted on a policy of no surrender. They prepared for a last-ditch defence on Japanese soil. Suzuki was forced by the army to promise that his government would continue the war 'to the bitter end'.

US marines on Okinawa, May 1945.

 ## Japan faces starvation

Koichi Kido was Lord Keeper of the Privy Seal, an adviser to the emperor, in Japan's imperial government. He later described why he wanted Japan to make peace in June 1945:

'The cities of Japan were being burned by bombings ... At least one city and at times two were being turned into ashes daily ... The weather moreover was especially bad in 1945. Consequently, rice crop forecasts were extremely bad. Everything became scarce. The food situation was gradually becoming worse and worse. Under such conditions even the soldiers had not too much to eat. There was nothing in Japan. Even we in the Imperial Household Department had only two sweet potatoes for lunch. With winter ahead, I said I cannot bear the responsibility for the lives of tens of millions of people dying a dog's death from hunger and exposure.' (Quoted in Giovanitti and Freed, *The Decision to Drop the Bomb*)

Harry S. Truman became President of the USA just as the war in Europe was coming to an end.

On 18 June, at a meeting at the White House in Washington, President Truman and his military leaders agreed to plan for an invasion of the southern Japanese island of Kyushu in November. It would be followed by an invasion of the main Japanese island, Honshu, in March 1946. This is exactly what most ordinary Americans and Britons had been led to expect. They knew the Japanese as an enemy who would rather die than surrender. They thought the war would last at least another year and be ended by an invasion of Japan that would cost many thousands of Allied lives.

But secretly, the Allied leaders had good reason to hope that an invasion would not be necessary and that the war would end soon. They knew things that the British and American public and ordinary soldiers did not. They knew that the Soviet Union had promised to declare war on Japan, adding its massive forces to the Asian battlefield. They knew that some Japanese were trying to start peace negotiations with the USA. And they knew that the first atomic bomb was almost ready for use.

The cost of an invasion

How many Allied soldiers would have died if Japan had been invaded? Henry L. Stimson, who was US Secretary of War in 1945, later claimed that half a million American lives would have been lost in an invasion. This helped to justify the decision to drop the atom bomb.

Historian Barton J. Bernstein disagrees. Bernstein claims that the US military planners preparing the invasion of Japan told the president to expect many fewer deaths. According to Bernstein, the planners said that about 25,000 Americans would probably die in the first invasion of Kyushu, and 21,000 in the follow-up invasion of Honshu. Bernstein writes: 'The myth of the 500,000 American lives saved thus seems to have no basis in fact.'

Of course, 46,000 lives is still a high number. And the number of Japanese killed in an invasion might well have reached half a million.

MAKING THE ATOM BOMB

It was in 1939, the year when the Second World War began, that scientists discovered the possibility of an atom bomb. Physicists had been carrying out experiments with atomic particles. They knew that a uranium atom could be split, releasing some of the energy in the atom's nucleus. If this splitting, or fission, became a chain reaction, a very large number of atoms would be split in a very short period of time. The result could be a massive explosion.

Albert Einstein. His Theory of Relativity (1905) explained that an enormous amount of energy was locked up in atoms.

All the major countries involved in the war had scientists who understood how a nuclear explosion could work. They also knew that the country that first made an atomic bomb could win the war. But no one knew if it was really practical to create this new weapon – if it would take five years, fifty years, or virtually for ever. In the end, it was only the USA who put enough resources behind an atom bomb project to make it work.

Race for the bomb

President of the USA, Franklin D. Roosevelt first heard of the idea of an atom bomb in October 1939. He was given a letter signed by Albert Einstein, one of the most famous scientists in the world. The letter explained that 'extremely powerful bombs of a new type' might be built. Einstein wanted to be sure that the USA, not Germany, would be

Brigader-General Leslie R. Groves.

first to have such a bomb. As another scientist, Rudolph Peierls, later explained: 'The thought of Hitler being in possession of such a weapon with nobody else being able to hit back was ... very frightening.'

Roosevelt set up a 'Uranium Committee' to back research into an atom bomb, but at first it had low priority. Once the USA entered the war, however, the situation changed. Scientists working in Britain had already discovered how an atomic explosion could be controlled, a vital step towards making the bomb. They gave their knowledge to the Americans. In December 1941 President Roosevelt launched the Manhattan Project, a breakneck race to make the bomb a reality.

The Manhattan Project

A multinational group of top nuclear scientists set to work under the command of Brigadier-General Leslie R. Groves, with Robert Oppenheimer as scientific director. They worked at a number of places across the USA, but primarily at Los Alamos in New Mexico. Los Alamos was the site of a ranch school in beautiful, wild country far from human habitation. The school was bought and a camp was built there that eventually

Los Alamos

Many scientists and technicians hesitated to go to Los Alamos when the Manhattan Project's scientific director, Robert Oppenheimer, told them what was involved. He later wrote:

'The prospect of coming to Los Alamos aroused great misgivings. It was to be a military post; men were asked to sign up more or less for the duration [of the war]; restrictions on travel and on the freedom of families to move about would be severe ... The notion of disappearing into the New Mexico desert for an indeterminate period ... disturbed a good many scientists, and the families of many more.' (Quoted in Giovanitti and Freed, *The Decision to Drop the Bomb*)

Refugees from Hitler

Many of the scientists who helped make the atom bomb were Jewish refugees from Germany. The German dictator Adolf Hitler hated Jews and blamed them for all the ills of the world. When he became Chancellor in Germany in 1933, Jewish scientists were driven from universities and their books were banned. Most fled to Britain or the USA. Edward Teller was a Hungarian Jew working in Göttingen University in Germany in 1933:

'It was a foregone conclusion that I had to leave. I wanted to be a scientist. The possibility to remain a scientist in Germany and to have any chance of continuing to work had vanished with the coming of Hitler. I had to leave, as many others did, as soon as I could.' (Quoted in Rhodes, *The Making of the Atomic Bomb*)

Teller played an important part in the US atom bomb project. If people like him had stayed in Germany, Hitler might have got the bomb first.

housed 6,000 people. Scientists, technicians and their families lived in a self-sufficient community, fenced in and closely watched by military men obsessed with security. The project developed in an atmosphere of total secrecy which many of the scientists found irksome. At government level too, code names were always used for the bomb, to cover what was going on – the British authorities referred to it in writing as 'Tube Alloys'.

Groves and Oppenheimer (left). When the first atom bomb was tested in July 1945, the steel tower from which it was hung was vaporized in the explosion. The two men are standing by its remains.

Building an atom bomb proved immensely difficult. The scientific and technical problems were daunting. Germany and Japan never came close to making the bomb, because they did not put enough resources behind the task. In the USA, President Roosevelt gave the project limitless money, hiding secret spending of $2,000,000,000 from Congress and the public. Huge factories were built to produce the types of uranium and plutonium needed. Eventually 200,000 people were working on the project. Because of the secrecy surrounding the bomb, most of them had no idea what they were making.

'Little Boy', the bomb dropped on Hiroshima, was 3 metres long and 70 centimetres in diameter. It weighed 4,080 kilograms.

Britain believed it had a half interest in the bomb project, because it had provided valuable information at the start and sent scientists to Los Alamos. At a conference in Quebec in 1943, Churchill and Roosevelt agreed that the bomb would never be used without British approval. But as time went on, the USA saw the bomb increasingly as its exclusive property. In the end, Britain's supposed veto over using the bomb was effectively forgotten.

At the end of 1944 General Groves was able to tell President Roosevelt with confidence that he would have the first atom bombs in the summer of 1945. The USA was making the bombs to be used, like any other

Scientists and the German threat

The scientists who helped make the atom bomb were mostly humane people opposed to war and destruction. But they were afraid that if they did not create the bomb, Nazi Germany might get it first. Otto Frisch, who worked on the Manhattan Project, wrote:

'Why start on a project which, if it was successful, would end with the production of a weapon of unparalleled violence, a weapon of mass destruction such as the world had never seen? The answer was very simple. We were at war and ... very probably some German scientists had had the same idea and were working on it.' (Quoted in Rhodes, *The Making of the Atomic Bomb*)

weapon in wartime. Almost everyone in the know simply assumed that once they were ready, they would be dropped on one of America's enemies. A special air squadron for atomic bombing was already being organized by Colonel Tibbets.

By 1945 there was no longer a race with enemy scientists. The USA now knew that Germany was not able to make its own bomb. But there was a race to have the weapon ready before the war ended. Germany and Japan were facing defeat. Many people involved in the Manhattan Project, including Groves himself, were desperately keen to have a chance to try the bomb out.

General Groves

Brigadier-General Leslie R. Groves, the director of the Manhattan Project, was a tough army officer raised in the American 'can-do' tradition. He rode roughshod over any person who wanted to question or delay the making and use of the atom bomb. He said later:

'From the day that I was assigned to the project there was never any doubt in my mind but that my mission ... was to get this thing done and used as fast as possible, and every effort was bent toward that assignment.'
(Quoted in Rhodes, *The Making of the Atomic Bomb*)

They were putting a huge effort into building it. If the war ended before it was used, they would feel that their effort was at least partly wasted. And they would find it hard to justify all the money that had been spent.

Planning the drop

In May 1945 the new president, Harry S. Truman, set up a committee to advise him on the bomb. Called the Interim Committee, it was chaired by the US Secretary of War, Henry L. Stimson. The Interim Committee discussed two possible ways of using the bomb against Japan without killing masses of civilians.

One idea was to drop the bomb in a deserted place where the Japanese could witness its power. Then the USA would threaten to use it for real unless Japan surrendered. The other idea was to give the Japanese advance warning of where the bomb was going to be dropped, so that they could move the population out of the area. But the committee did not think these ideas would work. All its members agreed that the bomb should be used against Japan without warning.

Henry Stimson, US Secretary of War.

Warning the Japanese

In May 1945 the Interim Committee discussed the possibility of warning the Japanese of where and when the bomb would be dropped. US Secretary of State James F. Byrnes, a member of the committee, opposed a warning. He later wrote:

'We feared that, if the Japanese were told that the bomb would be used on a given locality, they might bring our boys who were prisoners of war to that area. Also ... if we were to warn the Japanese ... and if the bomb then failed to explode, certainly we would have given aid and comfort to the Japanese militarists.'
(Quoted in Rhodes, *The Making of the Atomic Bomb*)

Another committee, the Target Committee, was set up to decide where the bomb would be dropped. General Groves, who chaired this committee, said that the bomb should be used against a military target. But he also argued that the target had to be big enough to show the bomb's full effect. This meant that the target would be a large city. The bomb also had to be used against a city that had not already been damaged by bombing. If the bomb was dropped on rubble and ruins, its effect would not be clear.

Hiroshima was quickly chosen as an ideal target because it was large enough and mostly undamaged. It was also flat, so the blast of the bomb would have its maximum effect. As a port and army base, Hiroshima had some military significance. Other targets were more difficult to choose. Nagasaki, the site of important factories, was only added to the list at the last moment. Its hilly terrain made it unsuitable for seeing the full effects of an atomic blast. The US air forces were ordered not to attack the chosen target cities, to keep them undamaged.

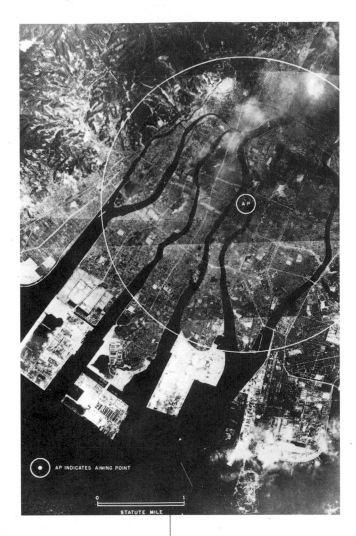

AP INDICATES AIMING POINT

STATUTE MILE

This aerial photograph of Hiroshima was taken after the bomb had been dropped. The large circle shows the area of the city which was destroyed.

The first atomic explosion

At the time that the Interim and Target Committees were doing their work, it was still not absolutely certain that an atom bomb would work. Two types of bomb were built. One, using uranium, was nicknamed Little Boy. This was the type dropped on Hiroshima. The other, using plutonium, was called Fat Man.

Scientists against the bomb

In June 1945, scientists in Chicago working on the Manhattan Project questioned the use of the atomic bomb. Led by Leo Szilard, James Franck and Eugene Rabinowitch, they expressed their views in a document called the Franck Report. It said:

'... it is not at all certain that American public opinion ... would approve of our own country being the first to introduce such an indiscriminate method of wholesale destruction of human life ... The military advantages and the saving of American lives achieved by the sudden use of atomic bombs against Japan may be outweighed by the ensuing loss of confidence and by a wave of horror and repulsion sweeping over the rest of the world ... From this point of view, a demonstration of the new weapon might best be made before the eyes of representatives of all the United Nations on a desert or barren island ...'

The Chicago scientists' views were never taken seriously by the political or military authorities.

The first atom bomb was tested at Alamagordo at 5.38 a.m. on 16 July 1945. A great fireball was seen. Two men at the nearest observation point, 10,000 metres away, were knocked down by the blast.

On 16 July 1945, a plutonium device was tested at Alamogordo in the New Mexican desert. Protected by little more than sun-tan lotion and dark glasses, 425 scientists and technicians saw the pre-dawn darkness lit up by a flash brighter than any light seen before on earth. Then the mushroom cloud, a brilliant purple colour, began its slow rise to over 12,200 metres above their heads. The explosion was much more powerful than most scientists had expected – equal to over 18,000 tonnes of TNT. At its centre, Ground Zero, it produced temperatures three times hotter than the core of the sun.

Physicist Isidor Rabi, who was at Alamogordo that morning, described the mixed reactions of the onlookers: 'Naturally, we were very jubilant over the outcome of the experiment ... We turned to one another and offered congratulations, for the first few minutes. Then, there was a chill, which was not the morning cold ...'

A memorial in the New Mexican desert.

66 'Death, the destroyer of worlds'

The atom scientists had mixed feelings as they watched the mushroom cloud of the first nuclear explosion rise above Alamogordo. They were glad to have succeeded, but afraid of the monster they had made. Robert Oppenheimer, the scientific director of the Manhattan Project, later said:

'We waited until the blast had passed, walked out of the shelter, and then it was extremely solemn. We knew the world would not be the same. A few people laughed, a few people cried. Most people were silent. I remembered the line from the Hindu scripture, the Bhagavad-gita: ... "now I am become death, the destroyer of worlds". I suppose we all thought that, one way or another.' (Quoted in Giovanitti and Freed, *The Decision to Drop the Bomb*) 99

DECIDING TO DROP THE BOMB

When the first atomic device lit up the New Mexican desert, on 16 July 1945, President Truman was at Potsdam, on the outskirts of Berlin, Germany. A coded message arrived from the USA, saying: 'Operated on this morning. Diagnosis not yet complete but results seem satisfactory and already exceed expectations.' Truman knew what it meant. He recorded in his diary: 'We have discovered the most terrible bomb in the history of the world.'

A general view of the Potsdam Conference.

The president was in Potsdam for a crucial meeting with his allies, British Prime Minister Winston Churchill and the wily Josef Stalin, ruler of the Soviet Union. They were discussing the post-war reorganization of Europe, and also the progress of the war with Japan. The president was visibly delighted when the news of the successful atomic test was brought to him. He felt it would help with the two major problems he faced. One was how to finish off the war with Japan. The other was how to deal with Stalin.

Facing up to Stalin

Britain, the USA and the Soviet Union had been allies since 1941. Josef Stalin, the ruthless Soviet dictator, had played a major part in winning the war against Germany. But now relations were turning sour. Churchill and Truman were trying to stop Stalin imposing Communist rule in Poland. They felt that the powerful new super-weapon would help them stand up to the Soviet Union. They also thought it might allow them to do without Stalin's help in the Far East.

'No special interest'

The Manhattan Project to develop the atom bomb had been kept a great secret. The Americans had especially not wanted their Soviet allies to know about it. At Potsdam Truman hoped to surprise and shock Stalin with the news. He wrote later:

'On 24 July I casually mentioned to Stalin that we had a new weapon of unusual destructive force. The Russian Premier showed no special interest. All he said was that he was glad to hear it and hoped we would make "good use of it against the Japanese".' (Quoted in Giovanitti and Freed, *The Decision to Drop the Bomb*)

We now know that Stalin's calm reaction was because he already knew all about the American bomb. Soviet spies were working inside Los Alamos and kept the Soviet leader informed of every development.

Left to right: Churchill, Truman and Stalin. Behind the scenes the relationship between them was less easy than it appeared.

'A miracle of deliverance'

In his memoirs, Winston Churchill described the reaction of British and American political and military leaders when they knew they had the atom bomb:

'We seemed suddenly to have become possessed of a merciful abridgement of the slaughter in the East ... To avert a vast, indefinite butchery, to bring the war to an end, to give peace to the world, to lay healing hands upon its tortured peoples, by a manifestation of overwhelming power at the cost of a few explosions, seemed after all our toils and perils a miracle of deliverance.' *(Triumph and Tragedy*, 1953)

Originally, one of Truman's main aims in coming to Potsdam had been to bring the Soviet Union into the war against Japan. If Stalin declared war on the Japanese, it would almost certainly shorten or even end the war. But now the USA had the atom bomb, Truman and his Secretary of State James Byrnes began to think differently: perhaps they could defeat Japan quickly without Soviet help. After all, if Stalin helped them, he was bound to demand a price.

At Potsdam, Truman's mind was divided on this matter. On 18 July Stalin agreed to attack Japan the following month. Truman wrote to his wife triumphantly: 'I've gotten what I came for – Stalin goes to war August 15 with no strings on it.' But secretly the president hoped the Japanese might surrender before the Soviets entered the war.

The Japanese at bay

Japan was close to surrender in July 1945. This was a secret known to Allied leaders, but not to the American or British public. The Allied leaders knew a great deal about what was going on in the Japanese government. American spies had cracked Japanese codes. They were able to intercept and read all the messages Japan sent to its ambassadors in foreign cities, including Moscow.

Japanese Foreign Minister Shigenori Togo was in favour of ending the war.

"SOMEBODY'S TALKING ABOUT US."

A cartoon from the *News of the World*, Sunday, 22 July 1945.

The secret messages showed that the Japanese government was split. Some of the inner cabinet, such as Foreign Minister Shigenori Togo, wanted to negotiate an immediate end to the war. Others, such as General Korechika Anami, the Minister of War, wanted to fight to a finish.

Emperor Hirohito backed those in favour of peace. He could see that Japan's position was hopeless. He wanted to use the neutral Soviet Union as a go-between in negotiations with the Allies. He planned to send a former prime minister, Prince Konoye, to Moscow to try to negotiate a peace deal. But these

The Japanese position

Spies intercepted the following message from the Japanese Foreign Minister Togo to Ambassador Naotake Sato in Moscow on 12 July:

'It is His Majesty's heart's desire to see the swift termination of the war ... However, as long as America and England insist on unconditional surrender our country has no alternative but to see it through in an all-out effort for the sake of survival and the honour of the homeland.'

peace feelers were hesitant and indecisive. No politician in Japan could commit himself too openly to making peace, because fanatical Japanese army officers were likely to assassinate anyone who did. And anyway, even those in favour of peace did not accept the Allied demand for unconditional surrender.

Getting Japan to surrender

The Allies were committed to 'unconditional surrender'. Truman felt that the American public would accept no less. But what exactly did unconditional surrender mean? Truman said publicly that it would not mean 'the extermination or enslavement of the Japanese people'. But did it mean that Emperor Hirohito had to go?

The Americans knew that this was a crucial point to the Japanese, who had been brought up to see their emperor as a sacred figure, descended from the Sun Goddess. If the Japanese thought the emperor could stay on the throne, they might surrender.

Emperor Hirohito in his coronation robes, 1926. He had chosen the word *Showa* ('enlightened peace') as the emblem of his reign.

The Potsdam Declaration

The Potsdam Declaration was intended to encourage the Japanese to surrender by a mixture of threats and promises, but it was too vague to do any good.

It did not promise to leave the emperor on his throne. Instead, it said that the military occupation of Japan would end when 'there has been established in accordance with the freely expressed will of the Japanese people a peacefully inclined and responsible government'.

It did not warn clearly of atomic attack. It ended: 'We call upon the government of Japan to proclaim now the unconditional surrender of all Japanese armed forces ... The alternative for Japan is prompt and utter destruction.'

Unfortunately, it was also a crucial point to much of the American public. They blamed Hirohito for the war and saw him in the same light as Hitler. According to an opinion poll, one in three Americans wanted Hirohito hanged. Truman did not feel he could promise to leave the emperor on his throne.

At the end of the Potsdam meeting, on 26 July 1945, the Allies made a dramatic public appeal for the Japanese to surrender. This is called the Potsdam Declaration. It did not offer to spare the emperor. Nor did it openly mention the new weapon that was about to hit Japan.

Japanese Prime Minister Suzuki rejected the Declaration at a press conference on 28 July. He said it was merely a 'rehash' of the previous demand for unconditional surrender. He said the Japanese government 'did not find any important value in it', and that the only possible course of action for the Japanese was to fight on. After this rebuff, the bombing of Hiroshima was certain to go ahead.

Eisenhower's view

General Dwight D. Eisenhower (above, right) was the Supreme
Commander of Allied forces in Europe in 1945 and a future president
of the USA. He was against the dropping of the bomb. He was with
Stimson when a cable came through confirming the success of the
bomb test, and Stimson told Eisenhower that they were going to drop
the bomb on the Japanese. Eisenhower later described his reaction:

'I was getting more and more depressed just thinking about it. Then he
asked for my opinion, so I told him I was against it on two counts.
First, the Japanese were ready to surrender and it wasn't necessary to
hit them with that awful thing. Second, I hated to see our country be
the first to use such a weapon.'
(Quoted in Rhodes, *The Making of the Atomic Bomb*)

Eisenhower also expressed this opinion to President Truman at
Potsdam, but his view was ignored.

No great decision

As the Allied leaders talked at Potsdam, Tibbets' bombers were already on the island of Tinian. The material for the first bomb was being shipped there for assembly on the spot. The plan was in place to drop the first atomic bomb on Hiroshima in early August. Only one of two things could stop it. Japan might surrender, or President Truman might give an order not to drop the bomb.

There was little likelihood that Truman would give such an order. There may not have been 'unanimous, automatic, unquestioned agreement' about dropping the bomb, as Winston Churchill later described in his memoirs. We know that General Eisenhower spoke against the use of the bomb, and other US military leaders may have expressed their doubts to Truman. But Truman wanted to make Japan surrender quickly without an invasion. He did not agonize over the dropping of the bomb. 'The atom bomb was no "great decision",' he later said. 'That was not any decision that you had to worry about.'

The order to use atom bombs on Japan was formally given on 25 July, the day before the Potsdam Declaration. It told Groves's team to go on dropping atom bombs until an order was given to stop.

Truman's diary

At Potsdam, President Truman kept a diary. On the evening of 25 July 1945 he wrote about the decision to use the first atom bomb. He said that it had been agreed that 'military objectives and soldiers and sailors are the target and not women and children ... The target is a purely military one.'

And yet Truman knew that the target was a Japanese city packed with civilian women and children. It was perhaps a fact that he could not face up to.

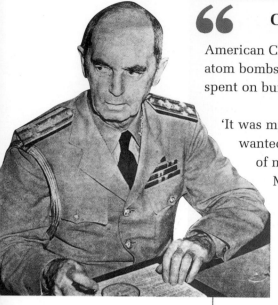

" Chief of Staff against the bomb

American Chief of Staff, Admiral Leahy claimed that the atom bombs were dropped to justify the $2,000,000,000 spent on building them:

'It was my reaction that the scientists and others wanted to make this test because of the vast sums of money that had been spent on the project. My own feeling was that in being the first to use it we had adopted the ethical standards common to barbarians in the dark ages. I was not taught to make war in that fashion ... ' (Quoted in Giovanitti and Freed, *The Decision to Drop the Bomb*) "

In 1945 Admiral William D. Leahy was the American Chief of Staff, the top military person under the president. After the war, he wrote that the atom bombs were 'of no material assistance in our war against Japan'.

Missing choices

Truman and other US leaders always said that they had had to choose between using the bomb and invading Japan at the cost of many US lives. Since the war, historians have pointed out other choices that the Americans had. They could have defeated Japan by a sea blockade and conventional bombing, without an invasion. Or they could have waited to see if the Soviet attack on Japan would finish the job.

" Would Japan have surrendered?

A question asked ever since the bombing of Hiroshima and Nagasaki is: Would the Japanese have surrendered even if the bombs had not been dropped? Or would the Allies have had to invade Japan to win the war? The official US Strategic Bombing Survey, written soon after the end of the war, stated:

'... certainly prior to 31 December 1945, in all probability prior to 1 November 1945, Japan would have surrendered even if the atomic bomb had not been dropped, even if Russia had not entered the war and even if no invasion had been planned or contemplated.'

No one can know if this opinion is true. "

Using the bomb against Stalin

Historian Gar Alperovitz has argued that the USA did not use atomic weapons in order to win the war against Japan. He claims that the bombs were dropped primarily to impress Stalin with American power and 'to force agreement on the main question in dispute' between the Soviet Union and the Western Allies, which was the future of Poland and Eastern Europe.

Most historians disagree with Alperovitz. They know that Truman and his colleagues saw the atom bomb as a help in standing up to Stalin. But they do not believe this is the main reason why bombs were dropped on Hiroshima and Nagasaki.

But at the time, Allied leaders did not see these things as alternatives to the bomb. They wanted to achieve a Japanese unconditional surrender as quickly as possible and with the least loss of Allied lives. They saw sea blockade, conventional bombing, Soviet attack and the atom bomb as things that together might get a result. Their strategy was described by Secretary of War Stimson as 'maximum force with maximum speed'.

Truman and his colleagues were not trying to avoid using the atom bomb. As Stimson explained after the war: 'No effort was made and none seriously considered to achieve surrender merely in order not to have to use the bomb.' Hiroshima was doomed.

'A tremendous shock'

The gentlemanly 77-year-old US Secretary of War Henry L. Stimson approved the use of the atom bomb against Japan. He later wrote:

'I felt that to extract a genuine surrender from the [Japanese] Emperor and his military advisers, there must be administered a tremendous shock which would carry convincing proof of our power to destroy the Empire. Such an effective shock would save many times the number of lives, both American and Japanese, than it would cost.' (Quoted in Giovanitti and Freed, *The Decision to Drop the Bomb*)

NAGASAKI AND SURRENDER

The first atom bomb was dropped on Hiroshima on 6 August 1945. Three days later a B-29 carrying a second atomic bomb lifted off from Tinian Island. This time it was a 'Fat Man' plutonium bomb, destined for the city of Kokura.

The 'Fat Man' bomb dropped on Nagasaki was 3.2 metres long and 1.5 metres in diameter. It weighed 4,500 kilograms.

The London *Evening News* reported the dropping of the second atom bomb, on Thursday, 9 August 1945.

This second mission did not go as smoothly as the first. It had been rushed because bad weather was on the way. The B-29, piloted by Major Charles W. Sweeney, flew through tropical rain squalls and lightning. When it reached Kokura the city was invisible beneath heavy cloud. Unable to drop its load, the B-29 headed on to its secondary target, the port city of Nagasaki. Here too there was heavy cloud. Short of fuel, the pilot could not wait. He had the choice of either dropping the bomb blind over the city or ditching it in the sea. He decided to drop it on the city.

The bomb landed 2.5 kilometres from its aim point at 11.02 a.m. on 9 August 1945. The effect was less devastating than at Hiroshima because Nagasaki is hilly. The hills sheltered much of the city from the blast. Most of the damage was limited to the valley where the bomb fell. But the horror was still on a massive scale. At least 35,000 people died in the bombing or soon afterwards. Some believe the true death toll was double that.

The road to peace

The Japanese government had not had time to react to the Hiroshima bombing. They had sent a military and scientific team to the city to report on what had happened. By the time they were sure that Hiroshima had been destroyed by an atom bomb, Nagasaki had also been hit. Meanwhile, on 8 August, the Soviet Union declared war on Japan. Soviet forces attacked the Japanese in Manchuria on the same day that Nagasaki was bombed.

View of Nagasaki after the bombing.

Street scene in Nagasaki, 8 September 1945.

Truman and the third atom bomb

On 10 August President Truman decided against dropping the third atom bomb. Secretary of Commerce Henry Wallace recorded in his diary:

'Truman said he had given orders to stop the atomic bombing. He said the thought of wiping out another 100,000 people was too horrible. He didn't like the idea of killing, as he said, "all those kids".'

PASTE THIS ON YOUR WINDOW!

This means
JAPAN SURRENDERS!

From page 1 of the *Daily Express*, 15 August 1945.

Both the atomic bombing and the Soviet offensive were disasters for Japan. But still members of the Japanese inner cabinet were split over whether to surrender. After a day of argument, they called in the emperor to decide on the issue. At 2 a.m. on 10 August, Hirohito came down on the side of surrender. The Japanese then told the Allies that they were ready to give in. They would accept the Potsdam Declaration as long as it 'did not prejudice the prerogatives of His Majesty as a Sovereign Ruler'. In other words, the emperor must stay on the throne.

President Truman and his advisers were themselves split over accepting this Japanese proviso. In their reply, they avoided the issue of the emperor's long-term future. They said that after the surrender Hirohito would be 'subject to the Supreme Commander of the Allied Powers', and that eventually the Japanese people would be able to choose their own form of government. This reply led to more fierce debates in the Japanese government. While they hesitated, massive US air attacks on Japan continued, some of the biggest of the war. But Truman had ruled out the use of the third atom bomb that was almost ready.

Finally, on 14 August, the emperor intervened again. He told the Japanese leaders they must 'bear the unbearable' and accept the Allied terms. He recorded a radio broadcast to inform his people the following day. Army officers attempted a military coup in Tokyo to stop the surrender, but they did not succeed.

The emperor's broadcast went out just before noon on 15 August. The Japanese people had never heard the emperor speak before and most did not understand his high-flown Japanese. But nonetheless the message got across. The war was over.

 The emperor's broadcast

In his radio broadcast Hirohito told his people:

'... the war situation has developed not necessarily to Japan's advantage ... Moreover, the enemy has begun to employ a new and most cruel bomb, the power of which to do damage is indeed incalculable, taking the toll of many innocent lives ... We have resolved to pave the way for a grand peace for all generations ...'

Emperor Hirohito and his wife in 1946.

 Hearing the emperor's voice

Kiyoshi Tanimoto, Japanese pastor of the Hiroshima Methodist Church, described in a letter how he went to Hiroshima railway station on 15 August to hear the emperor's broadcast. A crowd of people, most of them in bandages or standing with the aid of sticks, gathered around a loudspeaker in the ruins of the station.

'They listened to the broadcast and when they came to realise the fact that it was the Emperor, they cried with full tears in their eyes. "What a wonderful blessing it is that Tenno [the Emperor] himself call on us and we can hear his own voice in person ..." When they came to know the war was ended – that is, Japan was defeated, they, of course, were deeply disappointed, but followed after their Emperor's commandment in calm spirit, making wholehearted sacrifice for the everlasting peace of the world – and Japan started her new way.' (Quoted in John Hersey, *Hiroshima*)

Did the atom bombs make Japan surrender?

According to Japanese witnesses, the bombs helped those Japanese leaders who wanted peace to win their argument against the militarists, who wanted to fight on. Marquis Koichi Kido, adviser to the emperor in 1945, later said:

'The presence of the atomic bomb made it easier for us politicians to negotiate peace. Even then the military would not listen to reason.'

Hisatune Sakomizu, secretary to the Japanese cabinet in 1945, confirmed this:

'If the A-bomb had not been dropped we would have had great difficulty to find a good reason to end the war.' (Both quoted in Giovanitti and Freed, *The Decision to Drop the Bomb*)

Reactions to the bomb

The Japanese surrender came as a shock to most American and British people, both service personnel and civilians. They had expected the war to go on for months or even years. They were jubilant and deeply grateful for the atomic bombs. It seemed obvious that the bombs had ended the war. An American publication, *The New Republic*, used the headline: 'Thank God for the Atomic Bomb'.

An American soldier

Paul Fussell is now a well-known American writer. In August 1945 he was serving in the US army:

'I was a 21-year-old second lieutenant leading a rifle platoon ... When the bombs dropped and news began to circulate that the invasion of Japan would not, after all, take place, that we would not be obliged to run up the beaches near Tokyo assault-firing while being mortared and shelled ... we cried with relief and joy. We were going to live. We were going to grow up to adulthood after all.' (Quoted in Rhodes, *The Making of the Atomic Bomb*)

People were also amazed at what science had managed to do. The first press release from the White House on 6 August had called the bomb 'the greatest achievement of organized science in history'. This was a common view. However, many radio broadcasters and newspaper journalists also made the point that what had happened to Hiroshima could happen to New York or London in the future. Even as they celebrated the end of the war, people could see that dangers lay ahead.

The surrender ceremony on board the USS *Missouri*, 2 September 1945.

Just glad it was over

In August 1945, George MacDonald Fraser was in the British army, fighting the Japanese in Burma. In his book *Quartered Safe Out Here*, he recalled the reaction of his platoon to Hiroshima and Nagasaki:

'Like everyone else, we were glad it was over, brought to a sudden devastating stop by those two bombs that fell on Japan. We had no slightest thought of what it would mean for the future, or even what it meant at the time; we did not know what the immediate effect of those bombs had been on their targets, and we didn't much care ... our country had been hammered mercilessly from the sky and so had Germany ... we were not going to lose sleep because the Japanese homeland had taken its turn.'

8 October 1945: these children in Hiroshima wore masks against the smell of death in the city.

March 1946: new homes on plots cleared of rubble.

At the end of August Allied soldiers began to arrive in Japan to take over the defeated country. They could see the effect of the atomic bombs for themselves. Journalist Marcel Junod described the centre of Hiroshima in early September 1945 as a 'dead city' where 'absolute silence reigned'.

Radiation sickness

By September many of the survivors of the bombings were in the middle of a new nightmare. They had developed what was to be known as radiation sickness. About ten or fifteen days after the bombing they began to lose their hair. Diarrhoea and fever followed. They had lost the white blood cells needed to protect the body against disease. Many developed open sores. If the white blood cell count went too low, or the fever too high, they died. This happened to tens of thousands of people.

Writing home from Hiroshima

Osborn Elliot was an ensign on the USS *Boston* in 1945. He visited Hiroshima a few weeks after the Japanese surrender. He wrote in a letter home:

'How anybody was left alive, I do not know. But here and there, women and children were sitting on the rubble that was once their homes ... Many people had scars on their faces. We stared at them, and they gazed blankly back at us.' (Quoted in *Newsweek*, 24 July 1995)

The survivors were given no special help to rebuild their lives, either by the Allies or by Japanese officials. Within Japan, silence was swiftly drawn over the fate of the cities. Censorship imposed by the Allies prevented the Japanese press from making any mention of what had happened to Hiroshima and Nagasaki. Survivors were not allowed to tell their stories. The Allied authorities confiscated Japanese film of Hiroshima taken after the bombing.

September 1946: grandmother, mother and daughter, sole survivors of their family, gave up hope that they would be provided with a new home and left Hiroshima.

Outside Japan, both leaders of the great powers and ordinary citizens began to come to terms with living in the atomic age. What would it be like to live in a world menaced for ever more by the possibility of nuclear war? Were the ruins of Hiroshima and Nagasaki a vision of the future of the whole globe?

LIVING WITH THE BOMB

Danish physicist Niels Bohr argued for international cooperation to prevent a nuclear arms race.

Before the first atom bomb had been made, some people could already see that it was going to change the world. The Danish physicist Niels Bohr, who worked on the Manhattan Project, was one person who thought about the atomic future. In 1944 he tried to explain to President Roosevelt and Prime Minister Churchill what the risks were.

Bohr called on the USA and Britain to share the bomb with the Soviet Union. He said they should put atomic weapons under international control. He said that if the USA tried to keep the bomb to itself, other countries such as the Soviet Union would rush to make their own atomic weapons. A nuclear arms race would start that would be a disaster for humanity. Bohr and other scientists who argued in this way were ignored. What they feared is exactly what happened.

A different future

Some people found hope in the atom bomb. They thought it would force the world to turn to peace, because war had become unthinkable. Robert Oppenheimer, the scientific head of the Manhattan Project, took this view. In a lecture in 1946, he said:

'It did not take atomic weapons to make man want peace, a peace that would last. But the atomic bomb was the turn of the screw. It has made the prospect of future war unendurable. It has led us up those last few steps to the mountain pass; and beyond there is a different country.' (Quoted in Rhodes, *The Making of the Atomic Bomb*)

A MAD world

Until 1949 the USA was the only country in the world with atomic weapons. Then the Soviet Union exploded its own bomb. In the same year, the USA formed the North Atlantic Treaty Organization (NATO) with Britain and other European countries – a military alliance against the Soviet Union. In 1950, the Korean War broke out. A UN army led by the USA fought against Communist North Korea and China, which were backed by the Soviet Union. In 1955 the Soviet Union created its own military alliance, the Warsaw Pact, against the West. Although NATO and Warsaw Pact forces never fought one another directly, the two sides planned, plotted and manoeuvred against one another all around the world. This confrontation, called the Cold War, lasted for forty years.

Inevitably, the USA and the Soviet Union became involved in a nuclear arms race. Both sides made bigger and bigger bombs. In 1952, the Americans tested the first hydrogen bomb, which produced an explosion equivalent to over 10 million tonnes of TNT. That

November 1952: the first successful hydrogen bomb test at Enewetak Atoll in the Marshall Islands.

meant it was 500 times more powerful than the atomic bomb dropped on Hiroshima. By the start of the 1960s, the Soviet Union was testing bombs over a thousand times more powerful than the Hiroshima bomb. Meanwhile, Britain exploded its first atomic bomb in 1952 and its first hydrogen bomb in 1957. France and China joined the 'nuclear club' in the 1960s.

The Soviet Union paraded its missiles in Moscow, as part of celebrations of the anniversary of the Russian Revolution.

From the late 1950s, missiles were perfected that could carry nuclear warheads as powerful as hydrogen bombs to any city in the world. There could be no hope of defence against them. The missiles were kept in a constant state of readiness, so they could be fired at a moment's notice. The world was always only a few minutes from destruction. Peace was kept by the logic of MAD – Mutually Assured Destruction. Since both sides knew their cities could be wiped out in a day, neither could start a war. But there was always the risk that a nuclear war might start by accident, or that one side or the other might feel it had to launch a war to protect some vital interest.

In 1963 the USA and the Soviet Union agreed to stop carrying out nuclear tests in the atmosphere. The fallout from these massive nuclear explosions, carried out in the Pacific or in remote land areas such as Siberia, had created dangerous levels of radiation. But the number of nuclear weapons continued to increase. Despite agreements on arms limitation, by the 1980s there were about 50,000 warheads in the world's nuclear arsenals. They had an explosive force equal to 1,600,000 of the bombs dropped on Hiroshima. Some scientists said it was enough to end life on earth.

In the event, a nuclear war between the USA and the Soviet Union never happened. The Cold War ended in the late 1980s, when Mikhail Gorbachev led the Soviet Union to a new understanding with the USA. In the 1990s, the Soviet Union fell apart and ceased to exist as a single state. The number of nuclear weapons has been sharply reduced. But the risk of a nuclear war happening somewhere in the world will remain very real as long as such weapons exist.

Young people in Tokyo protested against French nuclear tests in the South Pacific, 1995.

Historians and the bomb

Immediately after the war, most American historians accepted the view that the atom bombs were dropped in order to end the war as quickly as possible. Then, in the 1960s, a more critical study of the evidence revealed other motives behind the bombings.

The first major 'revisionist', Gar Alperovitz, suggested the bombs were dropped primarily to impress the Soviet Union with American power. Other revisionists said that the need to justify the expense of building the bomb drove US leaders to use it. They also suggested that some people who had been involved in building the bomb just wanted a chance to try it out.

Most historians today feel that an invasion was not the only alternative to using the bomb. They think it was a mistake not to offer to leave the emperor on his throne. They feel that US leaders did not think hard enough about the suffering and death the bomb would cause. They recognize that the desire for revenge against the Japanese was a powerful motive. But they believe US leaders did genuinely hope that dropping the bomb would shorten the war.

America pleads not guilty

After 1945, there was no wave of guilt in the USA about the dropping of the atom bombs. Most Americans believed that the use of the bombs had been justified. They accepted the maths of war as presented by their leaders – more lives were saved by the bombs than lost. The USA never apologised to Japan for the bombings or admitted they might have been a mistake.

Yet the horror of what had happened in the two Japanese cities may have had a real effect on American leaders. Having seen what nuclear weapons could do, they were perhaps less likely to employ them. The USA did not use the atom bomb in the Korean War. Nor were nuclear weapons used in America's war in Vietnam in the 1960s and 1970s. Half a century after

the bombing of Hiroshima and Nagasaki, Little Boy and
Fat Man remain the only two nuclear weapons to have
been used in war.

In countries across the world, during the half a century
since the bombing of Hiroshima and Nagasaki, peace
groups have organized to oppose nuclear weapons. For
them all, the experience of the two Japanese cities in
1945 seemed a foretaste of what might happen in the
future to the whole planet.

London, 1961: Vanessa
Redgrave (left) and Bertrand
Russell (centre right) at an
anti-bomb demonstration.

World government

British philosopher Bertrand Russell became an ardent campaigner
against nuclear weapons. He believed that only a total change in the
world system of government could avoid a nuclear holocaust. In an
interview published in 1954, Russell said:

'I think the existence of the hydrogen bomb presents a perfectly clear
alternative to all the governments of the world. Will they submit
to an international authority, or shall the human race die out?'

Japan as an ally

After its surrender, Japan was taken over by Allied troops. Some Japanese were tried for war crimes, but the emperor was quietly left on his throne. In the 1950s Japan regained its independence and became an ally of the USA. Many survivors of Japanese prisoner-of-war camps were bitter to see Japan recover and grow rich on trade. But for the US government, the Soviet Union, not Japan, was now the enemy.

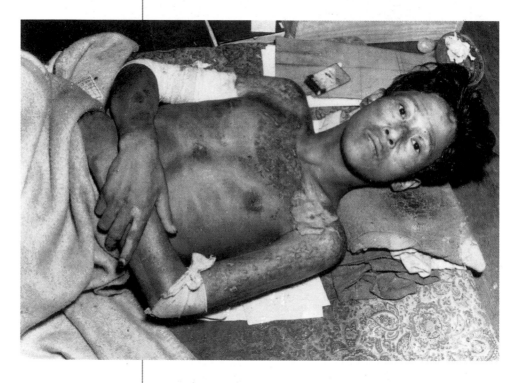

Hiroshima, 1947: a survivor showed her scars, almost two years after the atom bomb was dropped.

In the course of time, Hiroshima and Nagasaki became bustling cities again. They were rebuilt and soon had more people living in them than in 1945. The marks of the bombings remained most visible on the survivors, known in Japanese as hibakusha. Many had a special form of scar on their skin. All were scarred in their minds by what they had suffered.

Fortunately, the long-term effects of radiation were not as bad as once feared. The hibakusha were about ten per cent more likely than other people to die from leukemia and several other cancers. Many babies in the

womb at the time the bombs were dropped were harmed. But children born to hibakusha in later years have been normal. It appears that the harm of radiation will not be handed on from generation to generation.

In Hiroshima, the remains of the Industry Promotion Centre have been kept as a memorial, in the centre of the rebuilt city.

Nagasaki Harbour, 1996.

Coming to terms

A Peace Museum and Peace Park were opened in Hiroshima in 1955 to commemorate the bombing. Hiroshima Day, 6 August, is always observed there with ceremony. But the Japanese were slow to come to terms with the darker side of their own past. By concentrating on Hiroshima and Nagasaki, they tended to see themselves as victims of the war. They forgot their own aggression and war crimes. In 1995, for the first time, a Japanese leader apologised to the victims of Japan. On the fiftieth anniversary of the Japanese surrender, Prime Minister Tomiichi Murayama expressed 'feelings of deep remorse'. He offered a 'heartfelt apology' over Japan's actions in the war.

Prime Minister Tomiichi Murayama, 1995.

On Hiroshima day fifty years after the dropping of the bomb, 60,000 people stood for a minute's silence in the city's Peace Park. The city's mayor, Takashi Hiraoka, warned that as long as there were nuclear weapons, the story of Hiroshima could happen again. And 1,500 doves were released into the sky over the city as a symbol of hope and peace.

'Unbroken peace'

Sankiche Toge, a survivor of Hiroshima, wrote the most famous Japanese poetry about the atom bomb. The Prelude from his *Genbaku Shishu* (Poems of the Atomic Bomb) is engraved on a memorial in the Peace Park in Hiroshima:

Bring back the fathers! Bring back the mothers!
Bring back the old people!
Bring back the children!
Bring me back!
Bring back the human beings I had contact with!

For as long as there are human beings, a world of human beings,
bring us peace, unbroken peace.

Doves released above Hiroshima's Peace Park, 6 August 1995.

DATE LIST

1939

1 September — Second World War begins in Europe when Germany invades Poland.

1941

22 June — Germany invades the Soviet Union.

7 December — Japanese aircraft attack the US naval base at Pearl Harbor.

December — The Manhattan Project is started in the USA, with the aim of building an atomic bomb.

1942

15 February — The British base at Singapore surrenders to the Japanese.

March — President Roosevelt signs Executive Order 9066, under which Japanese Americans are moved to camps in the mid-west.

15-29 April — In the Bataan Death March in the Philippines, about 10,000 US and Filipino prisoners lose their lives.

4 June — The US naval victory over Japan in the battle of Midway turns the tide of the Pacific War.

November — Los Alamos is chosen as the main site for the Manhattan Project.

2 December — In Chicago, Enrico Fermi carries out the first controlled chain reaction, a major step towards creating an atomic bomb.

1943

14 August — British and American leaders meeting at Quebec agree that the atom bomb will not be used without British approval.

1944

7 July — The island of Saipan falls to the US Marines.

1945

14 February — The German city of Dresden is destroyed by RAF bombers.

19 February — US Marines land on the island of Iwo Jima.

9-10 March — US fire-bomb raid destroys much of Tokyo.

12 April — President Roosevelt dies. Harry S. Truman becomes US president.

8 May — Germany surrenders to the Allied forces in Europe.

21 June — The Americans take the island of Okinawa.

16 July — The first atomic device is exploded in the New Mexico desert.

17 July — The Potsdam Conference opens in the outskirts of Berlin.

26 July	In the Potsdam Declaration, the Allies call on Japan to surrender.		9 August	Soviet forces invade Manchuria.
6 August	An atomic bomb is dropped on the Japanese city of Hiroshima.		15 August	Emperor Hirohito of Japan broadcasts to his people, announcing the Japanese surrender.
8 August	The Soviet Union declares war on Japan.		2 September	Japan signs a surrender on board the USS *Missouri*.
9 August	An atomic bomb is dropped on the Japanese city of Nagasaki.			

RESOURCES

RECOMMENDED READING

John Hersey, *Hiroshima*, Penguin, 1986: Originally written in 1946, this is still the best book on the experience of Hiroshima from the point of view of the survivors.
Richard Rhodes, *The Making of the Atomic Bomb*, Penguin, 1988: This is the best account of the scientific achievements and personal struggles behind the making and dropping of the bomb.
Jonathan Schell, *The Fate of the Earth,* Macmillan, 1982: This sets out the anti-nuclear argument.
A.J.P. Taylor, *The Second World War*: The best short illustrated account of the war.
J.G. Ballard, *Empire of the Sun*: A novel about life as a prisoner of the Japanese, later filmed by Stephen Spielberg.
Norman Mailer, *The Naked and the Dead*: A heavy-weight novel that gives a good impression of the desperate fighting in the Pacific War.

FILMS

The Bridge on the River Kwai: This famous old movie by director David Lean, based on the novel by Pierre Boulle, portrays something of life as a prisoner of the Japanese.
Pica Don: A cartoon film by Japanese animator Renzo Kinoshita, showing the events of the Hiroshima bombing. Hard to find, but worth seeing.
Dr Strangelove: Or how I learned to stop worrying and love the bomb: A wonderful satire on the MAD world of the nuclear arms race, starring Peter Sellers.

SOURCES

The following were used as sources of information for this book:

Alperovitz, Gar, *Atomic Diplomacy: Hiroshima and Potsdam*, Pluto Press, London, 1994
Carey, John (ed.), *The Faber Book of Reportage*, London and Boston, 1987
Fraser, George MacDonald, *Quartered Safe Out Here*, Harvill, London, 1992
Len Giovanitti and Fred Freed, *The Decision to Drop the Bomb*, Methuen, London, 1967
Stephen Harper, *Miracle of Deliverance*, Sidgwick and Jackson, London, 1985
Hersey, John, *Hiroshima*, Penguin, 1986
Hogan, Michael J. (ed.), *Hiroshima in History and Memory*, Cambridge University Press, 1996
Richard Rhodes, *The Making of the Atomic Bomb*, Penguin, 1988
Russell, Bertrand, *Autobiography*, Unwin Paperbacks, London, 1978
Gordon Thomas and Max Morgan-Witts, *Ruin from the Air*, Hamish Hamilton, London, 1977
John W. Dower, *War Without Mercy*, Pantheon, New York, 1986

GLOSSARY

atom bomb or atomic bomb
a type of bomb in which the explosion is caused by splitting the nuclei of atoms – nuclear fission.

chain reaction
the process by which the splitting of one atom releases particles that split other atoms, which in turn release particles that split yet more atoms.

conventional bombing
the dropping of high explosive or incendiary bombs, not atomic or hydrogen bombs.

fission
the splitting of the nucleus of an atom to release energy.

gamma radiation
harmful radiation released during a nuclear explosion.

Ground Zero
the point on the ground directly beneath where an atomic explosion occurs.

hibakusha
the Japanese word for survivors of the Hiroshima and Nagasaki bombings.

hydrogen bomb
a type of bomb in which most of the energy for the explosion comes from nuclear fusion – one nucleus uniting with another.

kamikaze
a Japanese word meaning 'divine wind', used for pilots who carried out suicide missions during the Pacific War.

military coup
the takeover of the government of a country by some of the armed forces.

nuclear explosion
an explosion created by releasing the energy contained in the nuclei of atoms, as in an atomic bomb or a hydrogen bomb.

nucleus
the dense core of an atom. Plural: nuclei

plutonium
a metal found in small quantities in uranium ore. It is very suitable for fission, and is used in nuclear reactors and nuclear weapons.

Potsdam Conference
a meeting of the USA, Great Britain and the Soviet Union, held at Potsdam, near Berlin, in July 1945.

Potsdam Declaration
a statement issued at the end of the Potsdam Conference, calling on Japan to surrender unconditionally.

prime
to prime a bomb is to prepare it for dropping. If it is not primed, it will not explode.

revisionist
a term used for historians who disagree with the accepted view of what happened in the past.

TNT
a high explosive, trinitrotoluene. Nuclear explosions are measured as equivalent to the effect of tonnes of TNT. If a nuclear bomb is said to be a '10 megatonne' device, it has an explosive power equal to 10 million tonnes of TNT.

unconditional surrender
a total surrender, with no conditions attached.

uranium
a radioactive metallic element used as a source of nuclear energy.

INDEX

Aioi Bridge **5, 6, 29**
Alamagordo **30, 31**
Alperovitz, Gar **41, 54**
Anami, Korechika **35**
atom bomb **4, 5, 8, 22, 23, 24, 25, 26, 27, 28, 29, 30, 31, 34, 39, 40, 41, 42, 43, 44, 46, 47, 50, 52, 54**

B-29 **4, 5, 17, 42**
Bataan Death March **13**
Bernstein, Barton J. **22**
Beser, Jacob, Lt **8**
Bohr, Niels **50**
Britain **10, 12, 16, 24, 26, 32, 50, 51, 52**
Burma **18**
Burma railway **13**
Byrnes, James F. **28, 34**

Caron, Robert, Sgt **8**
China **10, 11, 14, 15, 16, 51, 52**
Churchill, Winston **11, 26, 32, 33, 34, 39, 50**
Cold War **51**

Downey, William **4**
Dresden **16**

Einstein, Albert **23**
Eisenhower, Dwight D., Gen. **38**
Elliot, Osborn **49**
emperor, Japanese **18, 36, 37, 44, 54, 56** (*see also* Hirohito)
Enola Gay **1, 4, 5, 9**

'Fat Man' **29, 42**
Ferebee, Thomas, Maj. **8**
France **10, 52**
Franck, James **30**
Franck Report **30**
Fraser, George M. **47**
Frisch, Otto **9, 27**
Fussell, Paul **46**

gamma radiation **9**
Germany **10, 12, 16, 20, 24, 25, 26, 27, 32**
Gorbachev, Mikhail **53**
Groves, Leslie R., Brig.-Gen. **24, 25, 26, 27, 29, 39**

Halsey, William, Admiral **19**
hibakusha **56, 57**
Hirohito, Emperor **10, 35, 36, 37, 44, 45**
Hiroshima **4, 5, 6, 7, 9, 26, 29, 37, 42, 43, 48, 49, 52, 53, 56, 57, 58, 59**
Hitler, Adolf **10, 12, 20, 24, 25, 37**
Honshu **6, 22**
hydrogen bomb **51, 52**

Indonesia **18**
Industry Promotion Centre **3, 57**
Interim Committee **28, 29**
Italy **12**
Iwo Jima **18**

Japan **10, 11, 12, 16, 26, 28, 32, 34, 37, 39, 40, 44, 49, 54, 56**

Japanese expansion **10, 11, 15, 18**
Jews **25**
Junod, Marcel **48**

kamikaze **18**
Koichi Kido **21, 46**
Kokura **42**
Korean War **51, 54**
Kuribayashi, Tadimichi, Gen. **18**
Kyushu **22**

Laurence, William T. **13**
Leahy, William D., Admiral **40**
Lemay, Curtis, Maj.-Gen. **19, 20**
Lewis, Robert, Capt. **8**
Leyte Gulf **18**
'Little Boy' **26, 29**
London **16**
Los Alamos **9, 24, 25, 26**

MAD (Mutually Assured Destruction) **52**
Manchuria **43**
Manhattan Project **24, 25, 26, 27, 33**
Manila **15**
Marianas **4**
Moscow **34, 35, 52**
Murayama, Tomiichi **58**
mushroom cloud **5, 8, 31**
Mussolini, Benito **12**

Nagasaki **13, 29, 42, 43, 49, 56, 57, 58**

NATO **51**

Nazis **10**

nuclear fission **23**

nuclear tests **53**

nuclear weapons **52, 53, 54, 55, 58**

Okinawa **20, 21**

Oppenheimer, Robert **24, 25, 31, 50**

Pacific **53**

Pacific War **18, 19, 20, 21, 22, 32**

Papua New Guinea **18**

peace groups **55**

Pearl Harbor **12, 13**

Peierls, Rudolph **24**

Philippines **13, 15**

plutonium **26, 29, 31**

Poland **10, 32, 41**

Potsdam Conference **32, 33, 34, 35, 37, 38, 39**

Potsdam Declaration **37, 39, 44**

prisoners-of-war, Japanese **13, 56**

Quebec Conference **26**

Rabi, Isidor **31**

Rabinowitch, Eugene **30**

radiation sickness **48**

Redgrave, Vanessa **55**

revisionists **54**

Roosevelt, Franklin D. **10, 11, 12, 14, 17, 20, 23, 24, 26, 50**

Rotterdam **16**

Russell, Bertrand **55**

Saipan **18**

Shanghai **14,1 5**

Siberia **53**

Singapore **13**

Soviet Union **12, 22, 32, 34, 35, 41, 43, 50, 51, 52, 53, 54, 56**

spies **33, 34, 35**

Stalin, Josef **32, 33, 34, 41**

Stimson, Henry **14, 17, 22, 28, 38, 41**

surrender, Japanese **44, 45, 46, 47**

Suzuki Kantaro, Baron **20, 37**

Sweeney, Charles W., Maj **42**

Szilard, Leo **30**

Target Committee **29**

Teller, Edward **25**

Tibbets, Paul, Col. **1, 4, 5, 8, 27, 39**

Tinian Island **4, 8, 39, 42**

Toge, Sankiche **58**

Togo, Shigenori **34, 35**

Tojo Hideki, Gen. **11**

Tokyo **17, 19, 44, 53**

total war **16, 17**

Truman, Harry S. **9, 20, 22, 28, 32, 34, 36, 37, 38, 39, 40, 44**

'Tube Alloys' **25**

unconditional surrender **12, 26, 37, 41, 44**

uranium **23, 26, 29**

Uranium Committee **24**

USA **10, 12, 14, 15, 16, 17, 22, 23, 24, 26, 28, 32, 34, 41, 50, 51, 53, 54, 56**

Japanese in **14**

Van Kirk, Theodore **8**

Vietnam War **54**

Wallace, Henry **44**

War, Second World **4, 5, 10, 12, 13, 16, 20, 23, 32**

Warsaw **16**

Warsaw Pact **51**